FORAGED FLOWER ARRANGING

A Step-by-Step Guide to Creating Stunning Arrangements
from Local, Wild Plants

REBEKAH CLARK MOODY

FLORAL DESIGNER AND
OWNER OF FORAGE & FLEUR

PAGE STREET
PUBLISHING CO.

PAGE STREET
PUBLISHING CO.

Copyright © 2017 Rebekah Clark Moody

First published in 2017 by
Page Street Publishing Co.
27 Congress Street, Suite 105
Salem, MA 01970
www.pagestreetpublishing.com

Distributed by Macmillan, sales in Canada by The Canadian Manda Group.

20   19   18   17   1   2   3   4

ISBN-13: 978-1-62414-364-9
ISBN-10: 1-62414-364-4

Library of Congress Control Number: 2016918570

Cover and book design by Page Street Publishing Co.
Photography by Grace Dinwiddie

Printed and bound in the United States

Page Street is proud to be a member of 1% for the Planet. Members donate one percent of
their sales to one or more of the over 1,500 environmental and sustainability charities across
the globe who participate in this program.

TO ALL THE MAKERS, CREATORS AND DREAMERS

Contents

Introduction

Nature is constantly changing and evolving. Every time you walk outside, something is slightly different. Spring is a time of growth. Summer is a time of fruition. Fall is a time of maturity. Winter is a time of rest and renewal. It is beautiful to see these changes happen before your eyes. The goal of this book is not just to teach you how to replicate a specific arrangement, but to empower you to take these skills and make them your own, regardless of your location. As a professional floral designer, I have had the opportunity to create many different arrangements, all leaning on foraging to provide a more natural look. I have foraged in the mountains of California, the moors of Scotland and my own backyard in Atlanta, Georgia. Every place is different, and I have learned new things each time. The biggest takeaway these experiences have given me is this: there is no right or wrong way to connect with nature. There is no perfect plant (except for honeysuckle, which comes pretty darn close on my list). While the end product is important and the reason we do it, I believe creating floral arrangements is about the journey. I have enjoyed many of the experiences and adventures I've had while foraging just us much as what those experiences have yielded. I may go in search of one thing and come back with something completely different. Why? Because nature is unpredictable and may have something better in store than what I had originally planned. It's those little surprises that I love, the gems of the hunt and the thrill of the unknown.

rebekah clark moody

The Basics of Foraging and Floral Design

My interest in foraging started with my work in floral design. At first, it was a means to an end. Now it has become my passion. Foraging allows you to create unique arrangements, and it can inspire an innate sense of wonder whenever you go outside. There is unending beauty in the everyday landscapes that others take for granted. One cannot help but admire nature's gift on that particular day and what one might be able to create with it. When I first started foraging, I had a minimal knowledge about plants, but since then my knowledge has grown. Even though I have learned a lot there is always still more to learn. One of my favorite things in foraging is finding new types of botanicals that are unfamiliar to me. It always keeps me on my toes. There is never a dull moment in foraging!

LESSONS IN FORAGING

We are lucky to live in a time when we can easily access all the necessities of life, but this has caused many of us to lose touch with the earth. We too often forget where things come from and when they naturally grow. There is something magical about being in tune with the growing patterns of a plant and being able to see how it changes over the course of a year. For example, a dogwood tree will start the year with bare branches. It is beautiful but austere. As temperatures start to rise, little blooms begin to pop open in magnificent splendor and are one of the most beautiful flowers nature gives us all year. As we enter into the warmer temperatures, the blooms die off, giving way to beautiful green foliage. As temperatures begin to cool, it produces beautiful multitoned autumnal foliage that can enhance almost any arrangement.

Plants are transient. They grow and change throughout the seasons. In those changes, with their elusiveness and limitations, we find beauty.

The most important lesson in foraging is to keep your eyes open. I cannot tell you how many times I have almost run my car off the road because I noticed something beautiful growing that I wanted to snip. I can often go to the same place on two different days and find a different selection of foliage and blooms. It is easy to get excited about the showy things, like flowers, but I implore you to look outside of that. Find beauty in the mundane. Find an interesting way to use something you typically think of as boring. It is always interesting to me how many people don't appreciate the plants that I cherish. They dislike them not because they are ugly, but maybe they are deciduous, maybe they are invasive or just maybe they are letting preconceived notions cloud their mind. There are no bad plants. Let me repeat that: there are no bad plants—except for the poisonous ones. Let's avoid those at all costs.

I've found that the best places to forage are abandoned properties and parking lots, as well as any overgrown spots along roads and trails. Look for areas where something is abundant and will not be missed if you take some. Make sure not to hack the plant. Try to cut in a place that will encourage regrowth, such as the main trunk of a branch, base of a branch or above a bud. Always ask for permission before cutting a plant in someone's yard. I have found people to be very amenable with items they have in abundance and have not been specifically curating.

In the summer, it is best to forage either early or late in the day when it is not too hot. The plants will hold up better if not cut during the heat of the day. Make sure to place your freshly cut plants in water as soon as possible. It is best to bring a bucket of water with you. Fill it with only 3 to 4 inches (7.5 to 10 cm) of water so there is not a mess to clean up later. Clean up your haul by cutting away any branches or leaves below the waterline; that way your water will stay clean, and whatever you have cut will last longer.

The best way to tell if something is hardy is to touch it. Hardier plants feel sturdy. Often the best indicator is whether the leaves feel tacky, since those typically do not last long once they're cut. A hardy plant feels a little waxy, not to the degree of a fake plant, but it feels firm. If something doesn't feel sturdy, cut it and test it out. Some things, like pokeweed, will shrivel up if not in water but can last for weeks when allowed to drink constantly. Sometimes I first pull a leaf off and see how it does outside of water. Hardiness can also vary depending on the time of year, varietal, climate and so forth. Be adventurous. It pays off in the foraging game. Living materials subject us to many constraints, but it is through those constraints that we can create unique pieces of art.

Foraging Do's and Don'ts

- Do cut at the main trunk of a branch, the base of a branch or above a bud.

- Do forage during the coolest parts of the day when possible.

- Do use loppers for larger branches.

- Do bring a water source when possible (wet paper towels for stems work too).

- Do be respectful of wildflowers because many are endangered.

- Don't cut in the middle of a stem or branch.

- Don't worry about cutting at an angle when foraging.

- Don't cut from cultivated sources or on private property without asking for permission.

- Don't remove more than 25 percent of the plant from its source.

A NOTE ON POISONOUS PLANTS

The main plants to avoid are poison ivy, poison oak and poison sumac. The rash and discomfort comes from skin contact with oils produced by these poisonous plants. The level of the reaction varies from person to person. I do not have a reaction when I touch poisonous plants, whereas my husband can be wearing gloves and still get an awful rash from them. Just because you don't react, and very few people are that lucky, doesn't mean you should interact with these plants. Still avoid them!

POISON IVY

- Ground cover, low shrub or vine growing up trees

- Green leaves in three stem clusters with pointed tips that become yellow and red in the fall

- Produces yellow-green flowers that transition to white-colored berries in the summer

POISON OAK

- Looks like oak leaves and grows as a shrub

- Often grows in clusters of three, but the clusters can also have five, seven or nine leaves

- Produces clusters of green, yellow or white berries

POISON SUMAC

- Grows in swampy locations as a woody shrub

- Can have pairs of seven to thirteen leaves

- Leaves can be red, yellow and pink in the fall and produce cream or yellow berries

ELEMENTS OF DESIGN

"A decorative arrangement of flowers is a work of art. It is a picture in which living line and living color form the artist's medium."

—Clarence Moores Weed

When creating an arrangement, there are many elements to keep in mind, most important are form, shape, line, color and texture. It is these elements that help form the principles of design, the arsenal of the designer. The great thing about designing floral arrangements is that there is truly no right or wrong way to do it. This book is designed to teach you how to create asymmetrical arrangements inspired by nature, but always keep in mind that you are the ultimate designer. Once you learn the rules and techniques, feel free to break them—all the best artists do!

PRINCIPLES OF DESIGN

Whether making an arrangement, creating a sculpture or painting on a canvas, there is a set of principles that artists follow, even if they're not aware of it. Even in nature, you will see a harmonious pattern to things that begs to be replicated. While these principles may seem initially abstract, they become clearer with time and practice. There are many principles in floral design, but the ones that are most applicable are balance and shape, movement, emphasis and unity.

BALANCE AND SHAPE

Balance is one of the most important principles of design. It can include physical and visual weight, color and texture. When creating an asymmetrical arrangement, it is important to make sure that the arrangement is balanced on both sides while not replicating the design. It can be easier to create balance within an asymmetrical design when working in odd numbers, but this can also be achieved by creating clusters of certain ingredients, rather than using them evenly throughout the arrangement.

To create an asymmetrical design, think of an inverted triangle, with lines (actual or perceived) creating the points of the triangle. Rather than creating lines that are equally spaced within the triangle, I try to use my lines to create different angles and play with the traditional shape. In almost every arrangement I create, there will always be a high point and a low point, helping to perpetuate the idea of a triangle or tripod. Keep in mind the overall size of your vessel so that your tallest stem is not more than one and a half times the height of your vessel.

MOVEMENT

All living things must have movement, even if it is only implied. This is especially true in the world of floral designing. Movement can be achieved through lines and colors. Curved lines can actually be curved (like honeysuckle), but they can also be implied. Most floral pieces have a straight stem, so do not display them directly in a horizontal or vertical direction when trying to create movement. Instead, place stems diagonally to create an implied movement. This can also be created through the foliage on the stem or by using multiple pieces and layering to get the overall shape. Imagine creating a graceful gesture sweeping through the arrangement.

Color is a great way to introduce movement. When looking at an arrangement, our eyes wander over it, and we observe the different elements. Including a gradation of color will automatically help by creating varying spots of interest. A beautiful way to convey this is to start with lighter color tones and have a pop of color in a specific spot.

EMPHASIS

Movement can help emphasize the focal point, the crescendo. The showstopper flower or foliage that excited you the first time you saw it is the piece that needs to be showcased. Creating contrast among other elements in your arrangement can do this. Repetition of this showstopper piece leading toward the focal point is another great option.

UNITY

It is important to create a state of harmony in an arrangement, otherwise it will appear incomplete. The eye must be able to settle and enjoy the floral piece. It needs to feel at ease. Sometimes having too much variety can be disruptive. The goal is to find completeness with no desire to change or add to the floral design. Often you will need to walk away from the arrangement and come back to it later. I will always find ways to continue to change or add to an arrangement, but taking a step back and revisiting it a little later often gives me a perspective that I did not have before, and then I am able to find unity.

Spring

Spring is such a special time of year! Nature begins to come out of dormancy, and the flowers and trees begin to bloom. Every day, a little more life and color come back into nature. By midspring, the world is in full bloom. Everywhere you look is covered in flowers, from the most delicate clematis to the ever-so-hardy azalea. Some of the flowers growing in your own backyard can be more beautiful than the most perfect peony, in my humble opinion. The deciduous foliage that has been absent is back and ready to be used. We begin the tutorials here because of the abundance that is available for all to forage, no matter your location.

JAPANESE MAGNOLIA IKEBANA ARRANGEMENT

These blooms are like tiny dancers; let them steal the show. They convey movement, unlike most flowers, and look lovely through every stage of their life. Placing the blooms anywhere with a breeze, even if it's just a vent, will help them come to life, and they will put on a show for you. The style of ikebana floral design is about creating with less and letting those stems speak. The tallest piece symbolizes heaven, the second is earth and the third is humanity.

PLANTS
- Japanese magnolia blossoms

SUPPLIES
- Floral shears
- Putty adhesive or super glue
- Floral frog
- Oval bowl

FORAGE

1. When foraging Japanese magnolia, keep a few things in mind. First, make sure to cut pieces in varying states of growth, from the tightly closed buds all the way to the completely open blossoms. Second, cut more than you think you need because Japanese magnolia is very delicate, and the petals will fall off as you forage and arrange. While there is nothing out there quite like Japanese magnolia, dogwood or cherry blossoms are lovely arranged in an ikebana style.

(continued)

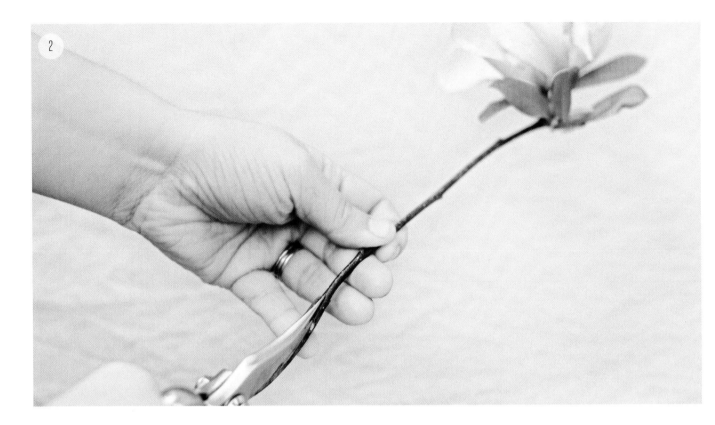

PREPARE

2. Cut a single slit in the bottom of the stem to allow it to drink more water. It will also make it easier to put in the frog. Take some waterproof floral putty and adhere the frog to your oval bowl slightly off center.

ARRANGE

3–4. The branches are delicate and have wonderful natural curves that create beautiful movement. Begin by placing the first two or three branches to create a triangle shape. Sometimes you can find pieces that split and naturally create the shape you are hoping to achieve, and it is magical. Once the overall shape is created, softly fill in by adding lower pieces, keeping in mind the original axis (shape) so you don't add them at an angle that will compete.

DISPLAY AND CARE

5. This is my favorite type of arrangement to have around my house. Even as it decays, it is beautiful, and I don't want to say goodbye. I like these kinds of arrangements in a highly visible place, such as on an entryway table or centerpiece in your home. Cover the frog and base of the branches with water. Replenish the water every few days.

AN ODE TO DOGWOOD:
SIMPLE DOGWOOD AND FORSYTHIA ARRANGEMENT

Here in Georgia, dogwood blooms start to open in late March and are in full bloom by early April. It is a gorgeous sight and takes my breath away every year. They are so wonderful to use when arranging because they are delicate, have a beautiful shape and add interest to something that could otherwise be bland. The forsythia adds a nice contrast to the overall look and is a fun addition to this arrangement.

PLANTS

- Honeysuckle
- Dogwood blooms
- Dogwood branches
- Forsythia blooms

SUPPLIES

- Floral shears
- Bucket
- Floral foam
- Knife
- Small urn

FORAGE

1. Find a base green; I used honeysuckle. Cut seven pieces of the honeysuckle. Cut three to five pieces of dogwood at different stages, some in full bloom and some with buds. The offshoots can be cut and used as smaller pieces in the arrangement. A colorful small bloom, like forsythia, will help add a little interest. Cut a few handfuls of the forsythia blossoms. Keep in mind the size of your urn and cut some pieces approximately twice its size so you have a little length to work with.

PREPARE

2. Cut the bottom of the stems and branches, and put them in clean water so they can drink prior to being arranged. The dogwood will need to be cut into smaller, more manageable pieces for the arrangement. A single cut up the center will help the stem drink more.

3. Fill a bucket with water and place the foam on top of the water. Be careful not to submerge the foam; just let it float and naturally soak up the water. After the foam has sunk to the bottom and darkened, use a knife to cut it to size and place it in the urn.

(continued)

ARRANGE

4–5. Take the honeysuckle, and start with three pieces to create a triangle shape. Continue to build out the shape.

6. Use the budded dogwood branches next, taking the shape out a little farther. Add small groupings (around three to five blooms) of dogwood throughout the arrangement. To finish, add a few pops of colorful forsythia blossoms.

DISPLAY AND CARE

7. This arrangement looks great as a statement piece, despite its size. Cut dogwood does not last very long, so it is best for this arrangement to be enjoyed as much as possible. Top the foam off with water every few days.

BLOOMING BRANCH AND
HONEYSUCKLE ARRANGEMENT, IKEBANA STYLE

One of the most inspiring things about early spring is the delicateness of the blooms just when they start to open. Very little interrupts the softness and color coming to the stern branches. This arrangement is inspired by the subtleness of nature when things are starting to flourish. This arrangement will make you feel like a fine artist, allowing you to focus on the small details and let them shine.

PLANTS

- 'Forest Pansy' redbud or another branch with delicate blooms
- Honeysuckle

SUPPLIES

- Floral shears
- Small floral frog
- Super glue or putty adhesive
- Shallow compote bowl

FORAGE

1. Find a selection of blooming branches. I used 'Forest Pansy' redbud, which actually has purple-hued blooms despite the name. Also, look for a green vine to complement the branches. Honeysuckle is what I used, but jasmine or another vine would also look great. To do this arrangement, only three stems of each piece are required, but gather a few extras to have options when selecting. The longest piece should be no longer than 3 feet (91.5 cm).

PREPARE

2. Adhere the floral frog to the compote bowl. I suggest using super glue, but waterproof putty is a great choice for a less permanent option. Once the frog is secure, fill the bowl with a light covering of water, touching the top of the frog.

(continued)

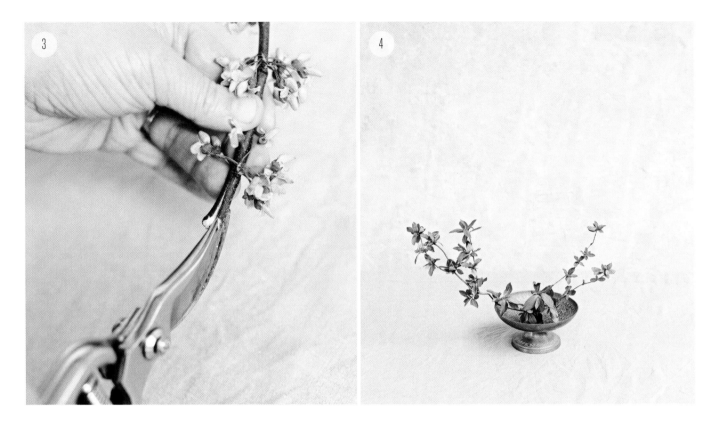

3. Trim your branches to the desired height. When working with a frog, it is sometimes helpful to cut a slit on the bottom of the branch so the pins can hold it more securely. It also helps the branch absorb more water.

Make sure to have three segments. In the ikebana style of floral arranging, the overall height can vary. Typically the tallest is one and a half times the size of the bowl, in this case the compote, and represents heaven. The second piece is three-fourths the size of the first and represents Earth. The final piece is three-fourths the size of the second and represents humanity. While I did not measure and adhere to these exact sizes, it is good to keep this guideline in mind while designing your arrangement.

ARRANGE

4–5. First, add three pieces of the honeysuckle. Pick pieces that have a lot of shape and movement. Arrange them in an upside-down tripod or triangle, one going diagonally to the left, one diagonally and slightly toward the back on the right and one diagonally and slightly toward the front on the right, each piece being slightly shorter than the last. Mirror this technique with three redbuds while weaving through the honeysuckle, creating a natural look.

6. If the frog is still visible, use a few small pieces of honeysuckle to cover it up.

DISPLAY AND CARE

7. This sort of arrangement needs to be placed in a space without many distractions such as on a side table against the wall or in front of a window. Make sure the bottom of the stems are covered with water and refresh with new water every few days.

LARGE BLOOMING URN ARRANGEMENT

There are days when I go out, and I cannot contain my excitement for everything growing. During the short time of year when all the early blooming trees are at their best, I want to bring some of them inside to brighten my house and allow them to mingle in a statement piece. Take advantage of these beautiful blooms and have some fun!

PLANTS

- Honeysuckle
- Cherry blossoms
- Pink Chinese fringe
- 'Forest Pansy' redbud
- Bradford pear blossoms
- *Elaeagnus* (silverberry)

SUPPLIES

- Floral shears
- Bucket
- Floral foam
- Knife
- Garden urn

FORAGE

1. Look for a mix of greenery and blooming branches. Early spring offers many delicate small blooms on one stem. This arrangement used an assortment of pinks (cherry blossom and Chinese fringe) and purples ('Forest Pansy' redbud), with a hint of white (Bradford pear). All the elements could easily be substituted, depending on availability and what grows locally. Just make sure to forage hardy greenery and blooming branches. Grab a large bunch of the *Elaeagnus* and pink Chinese fringe foliage because they will be the base and will really help build the arrangement. Three to five branches of each bloomer will suffice; cut more of each if you are using less overall variety.

PREPARE

2. Organize the foliage by type and edit the branches by removing any leaves or stems that will not be visible or will get in the way of the arrangement structure. This will allow for easier placement later.

3. Fill a bucket with water and place the floral foam on top of the water. Be careful not to submerge it; just let it float and naturally soak up the water. After the foam has sunk to the bottom and darkened, place the floral foam in the bottom of the garden urn.

(continued)

Tip: If needed, you can place something inside the urn to raise the foam closer to the surface.

ARRANGE

4–5. Grab a handful of your base green and get started by building out your initial triangle shape. It will be the inspiration for the rest of the arrangement. This arrangement used six pieces of *Elaeagnus*, each varying in shape and size. Continue with the next green, and mimic the original shape, tucking some pieces in deeper and having some go out farther.

6. It is really easy to be tempted to use a piece that has multiple offshoots because it automatically has a good shape. The problem with this is that all the offshoots may crowd the arrangement. It is better to edit a branch where it is needed to create a beautiful composition rather than using the whole piece. If you need to cut it out, do it. Tough love is necessary.

7–8. Once the greenery is built out, start adding the flowering branches. Allow them to be longer than the rest since they are the showstoppers. Also, use shorter branches and tuck them in. Once the overall look feels full, add a hint of the honeysuckle vine to add a wild component.

DISPLAY AND CARE

9. This arrangement needs to be front and center; showing off is the name of its game. I recommend putting it on a mantle or on a table in an entryway.

Blooming branches do not have a long life span, especially once cut. To help extend the life of the arrangement, make sure it is well hydrated by adding water to the urn regularly and spraying the blossoms with water.

AN ODE TO DOGWOOD: IN GOOD COMPANY

The only thing better than dogwoods and Japanese magnolias separately is pairing them together! The short period when they are both blooming may be my favorite time of year. Why would you leave them outside growing separately when you can create something beautiful to enjoy inside?

PLANTS

- *Elaeagnus* (silverberry)
- Dogwood blossoms and buds
- Japanese magnolia blossoms and buds

SUPPLIES

- Floral shears
- Wire cutter
- Chicken wire
- Urn
- Waterproof tape

FORAGE

1. Gather three medium-size bunches of each of the plants. Keep in mind you'll need a variety of heights. Sometimes it is easiest to cut them all longer than you would think, and then shorten them when you get home. I used *Elaeagnus*, but any hardy greenery will work well for this arrangement.

PREPARE

2. Clean up the branches by separating the offshoots into smaller pieces, and then putting them in clean water.

3. Use a wire cutter to cut a square of chicken wire twice the size of the urn opening, roll it into a ball and place it inside the urn. Put a piece of waterproof tape across the top of the urn to keep the chicken wire in place. Once the urn is ready, fill the majority of it with water.

(continued)

ARRANGE

4–6. Create a base layer of *Elaeagnus* with a high, medium and low point. Chicken wire is a little difficult to work with at first because things will shift as you work. As you build the foundation, the branches will be reinforced and start to stay in place. Take your dogwood blossoms and buds and add to the shape, continuing with the high, medium and low points. Add some magnolia to the mix, mimicking the shape.

DISPLAY AND CARE

7. This floral piece is perfect on an entryway table. It is the first thing guests will see when they walk in your front door. Refresh every few days with water.

LIGHT AND AIRY ARRANGEMENT

Pittosporum is an absolute dream to use; it lasts forever and is wonderful in most arrangements. It is a favorite of mine; I never seem to tire of using it. I try to think of new and creative ways to add pittosporum to a floral design. In this arrangement, it feels fluffy and light, allowing the other plants to shine. The abelia also achieves that look and it has small buds, making it a win-win.

PLANTS

- Pittosporum
- Abelia
- Hydrangea

SUPPLIES

- Floral shears
- Alum
- Bucket
- Floral foam
- Knife
- Goblet vessel

FORAGE

1. Cut fifteen to twenty stems of pittosporum in varying heights. Cut a few handfuls of abelia, making sure to get some with blossoms. Cut five to seven pieces of hydrangea. If pittosporum is unavailable, make sure to substitute with something else that will not visually weigh down the arrangement; honeysuckle is always great for that.

PREPARE

2. Trim the branches and stems at an angle, and put them in clean water for at least an hour so they can drink prior to being arranged. Prior to arranging, dip the bottom of the hydrangea stems in ½ inch (1 cm) of alum, a powder you can find in the spice section of a grocery store. This will help keep them from wilting.

3. Fill a bucket with water and place the foam on top of the water. Be careful not to submerge it; just let it float and naturally soak up the water. After the foam has sunk to the bottom and darkened, use a knife to cut it to size and place it in the goblet. Because of the shape of the vessel, the foam is inconspicuous so covering up is less of an issue.

(continued)

8

ARRANGE

4–7. Start with the pittosporum, creating an upside-down
triangle with one side longer than the other. Continue
to fill in while maintaining an airy shape. This can be
accomplished by placing pieces at varying heights and
thinning out the leaves where necessary. Fill with abelia,
putting the pieces in rhythm with the shape, but each
one slightly shorter. Finish with a mix of hydrangea
throughout, placing some tucked in the middle and some
farther out.

DISPLAY AND CARE

8. Place this arrangement somewhere simplistic, and allow
it to shine. The foam should be lightly watered every
few days. This arrangement is still pretty without the
hydrangeas after they begin to wilt.

CHINESE FRINGE ARRANGEMENT

Simplicity is often best in arranging. It allows the designer to truly focus on the raw materials and make something uniquely beautiful. Always be on the lookout for these rare pieces that you can turn into magical arrangements.

PLANTS

- Chinese fringe tree

SUPPLIES

- Floral shears
- Glass pitcher, preferably with a small mouth

FORAGE

1. Cut a mix of blooms and foliage from a Chinese fringe tree. Many pieces will have both on one stem, which is ideal. A smoke bush or any other mix of leaves and textural elements will achieve a similar look.

PREPARE

2. Clean the pitcher and fill with water.

3. Groom the branches by removing any dead leaves that will be below the waterline, and put them in clean water.

(continued)

ARRANGE

4–6. Start with two branches leaning in different directions. A small-mouthed pitcher is easiest to use because the stems will not easily come out or shift while you work. Continue to add pieces while creating an infrastructure of intertwined stems to help them stay in place. Next, you can add the final front and back pieces.

DISPLAY AND CARE

7. This arrangement is beautiful in a kitchen or living room area. If the water starts to look dirty, change it out with fresh water.

SOFT SPRING ARRANGEMENT

I love to find unique vessels for my flower arrangements. They add character and individuality to a floral design. My favorite place to find different vessels is at secondhand shops, which is where this southwestern pitcher was acquired. Always pick a vessel that will complement your selection of foraged material. In this arrangement, the soft tones of the flowers do not distract from the decoration on the pitcher, but instead complement it beautifully.

PLANTS

- Honeysuckle shrub
- Lacecap hydrangea
- Spirea

SUPPLIES

- Floral shears
- Alum
- Bucket
- Floral foam
- Knife
- Secondhand pitcher

FORAGE

1. Find a base green; I used the shrub varietal of honeysuckle. It still has the soft green foliage, but it does not grow in a vine. If you are lucky enough to have access to any hydrangea, get it! It is such a special bloom and can last up to a week with care. Spirea can be hard to find at times and can easily be substituted with a different delicate bloom or a vine-like green. A few handfuls of everything should suffice.

PREPARE

2. Clean your branches by removing excess foliage and immediately put them in water. Allow the hydrangea to drink for at least an hour before you start to arrange. Prior to arranging, dip the bottoms of the hydrangea stems in ½ inch (1 cm) of alum (a powder found in the spice section of the grocery store). This will help extend its life.

3. Fill a bucket with water and place the foam on top of the water. Be careful not to submerge it; just let it float and naturally soak up the water. After the foam has sunk to the bottom and darkened, use a knife to cut it to size and place it in the pitcher.

(continued)

ARRANGE

4–6. Take the base green and create the look of offshoots growing off one branch by layering the individual branches at different heights and lengths. Do not layer too heavily; the other ingredients will also have foliage, and they will compete for space in the arrangement. When adding in the hydrangea, create a V from three pieces. The final step is to add the spirea (or something else light and airy). Rather than editing the piece by removing the tiny offshoots as I normally suggest, I chose to keep them intact so the arrangement has a unique high point.

DISPLAY AND CARE

7. I love these types of perky arrangements in a bedroom; they can cheerfully greet you as you start the day. If the hydrangea starts to look sad, you can immerse the whole piece in water to help it perk up. Top off the foam with water every few days.

AN ODE TO DOGWOOD: THE LONER

There is nothing more beautiful than a simple dogwood arrangement. There is a lot going on in each flower on each stem that it creates a wonderful impact without much effort. Have I turned you into a dogwood lover yet?

PLANTS
- Dogwood blooms

SUPPLIES
- Floral shears
- Bucket
- Floral foam
- Knife
- Brass vessel

FORAGE

1. Cut around five branches of dogwood blossoms. A variety of heights and sizes are preferable. Any other beautiful blooming branch could be used if dogwood is not easily foraged.

PREPARE

2. Cut the branches at an angle, and put them in clean water so they can drink prior to being arranged.

3. Fill a bucket with water and place the foam on top of the water. Be careful not to submerge it; just let it float and naturally soak up the water. After the foam has sunk to the bottom and darkened, use a knife to cut it to size and place it in the vessel. The less conspicuous the foam, the easier it is to make the arrangement.

ARRANGE

4. Start with the first piece coming out of the vessel at an angle toward the left. Fill in with a few small pieces in the front and then add another large piece emerging from the right side of the vessel. More may be added depending on the size of each piece. Don't overfill; just make sure to fill in any holes.

DISPLAY AND CARE

5. This arrangement looks great as a statement piece despite its modest size. Cut dogwood does not last very long, so it is best to be enjoyed as much as possible. Top off the foam with water daily, since the dogwood is so delicate.

SMALL CLUSTER OF BUD VASES

Do you have guests showing up at the last minute? Are you quickly trying to make a space feel alive? Not a problem. This is an arrangement you can do in just a few minutes, but it adds a ton of character to any space.

PLANTS
- Dogwood blooms
- Lacecap hydrangea
- Spirea

SUPPLIES
- Floral shears
- Glass bottles

FORAGE

1. Cut small lengths of each floral piece, and make sure they range in size but are no longer than 1 foot (31 cm). I used dogwood, hydrangea and spirea, but you can experiment with whatever is growing near you and excites you. This is a great way to test out the hardiness of a plant without having it potentially wilt or die in your arrangement.

PREPARE

2. Trim the branches and remove anything that will be below the waterline. Put them in a small container filled halfway with water while gathering the bottles.

(continued)

ARRANGE

3–6. Take the little pieces and put them in the bottles. You can use a single stem or multiples in one bottle. This is a great time to play around with things you may not normally use and see how you like them in your house.

DISPLAY AND CARE

7. These little arrangements can be scattered around the house or in a cluster on a table. Change the water every few days.

AN ODE TO DOGWOOD: PRETTY IN PINK

Any chance you have to arrange with dogwood, take it! Wait, I may have mentioned that already, but it is because dogwood truly is wonderful. Ask any floral designer, and they will agree. This pink varietal is fun and less common than the white that we have already used.

PLANTS

- Lacecap hydrangea, with more greenery than blooms
- Forsythia foliage
- Wild roses
- Pink dogwood blooms

SUPPLIES

- Floral shears
- Alum
- Bucket
- Floral foam
- Knife
- Garden urn

FORAGE

1. Cut around five branches of lacecap hydrangea that vary in size. Focus on ones with more foliage than blooms. A handful of each of the other ingredients—forsythia foliage, wild roses and dogwood blooms—should be enough for the rest of the arrangement, but a few extras are always handy.

PREPARE

2. Trim the branches at an angle, and put them in clean water so they can drink prior to being arranged. Allow the hydrangea to drink for at least an hour before you start to arrange. Prior to arranging, dip the bottom of the hydrangea stems in ½ inch (1 cm) of alum (a powder found in the spice section of the grocery store). This will help extend its life.

3. Fill a bucket with water and place the foam on top of the water. Be careful not to submerge it; just let it float and naturally soak up the water. After the foam has sunk and darkened, use a knife to cut it to size and place it in the garden urn.

(continued)

ARRANGE

4–8. Start with the hydrangea by creating a V, and then place a shorter piece in the middle to break it up. Add the few pieces of forsythia foliage to continue building out the shape. Add the roses in a triangle pattern, leaving plenty of room for the dogwood. With the wild roses, I left the foliage on to add another leaf shape. Add the dogwood; try not to crowd the wild roses, but rather add in the empty space.

DISPLAY AND CARE

9. This arrangement is to be treasured, as it will last only for a short time. It would be cute on a side table or in a powder room. Refresh every few days with water.

SIMPLE MAGNOLIA ARRANGEMENT

Magnolias are arguably the most iconic flower of the South. These deciduous trees offer beautiful blooms and a delicious fragrance. It is no wonder that they are beloved. The best thing about arranging with them is the scent that will overtake your home. No perfume or candle can compete with the real deal.

PLANTS

- Magnolia blooms in different stages
- Magnolia foliage
- Chinese privet

SUPPLIES

- Floral shears
- Bucket
- Floral foam
- Knife
- Compote

FORAGE

1. Cut a few magnolia branches with big blooms, a few with blooms that are not as open and five to seven branches with just foliage. It is easier to arrange with them separately, rather than all together on one branch. Cut a handful of Chinese privet or another branch with soft blooms or textural bits.

PREPARE

2. Trim the branches at an angle, and put them in clean water so they can drink prior to being arranged.

3. Fill a bucket with water and place the foam on top of the water. Be careful not to submerge it; just let it float and naturally soak up the water. After the foam has sunk to the bottom and darkened, use a knife to cut it to size and place it in the compote.

(continued)

ARRANGE

4–6. Start with placing two pieces of foliage on opposite sides, one toward the right front and one toward the left back. Continue to fill in with the leaves on either side. Begin placing the blooms. Because of the size of magnolia blossoms, not many are needed; I used only two. While three blooms would have looked nice, I flipped the foliage on the right side to create some lighter tones to balance out the blooms. Lastly, add the Chinese privet to lighten up the weight of the arrangement.

DISPLAY AND CARE

7. I love to use this arrangement as a centerpiece for outdoor gatherings. It adds an air of sophistication to a simple outdoor picnic table. There is not much to be done to extend the life of this arrangement. Magnolia foliage will last a while, but the blooms quickly start to brown. Luckily, they produce such a lovely scent that you won't even mind. Refresh the water every few days.

Summer

As the heat rises and summer comes around, many of the springtime blooms have left, but we are given the most interesting types of wildflowers, which usually stick around until the first frost. Foliage and textural elements are everywhere you look and offer so much excitement—have I mentioned honeysuckle? Summer is my favorite time to explore and experiment with the newfound flora. My current favorite summer ingredient is pokeweed, and I would love for you to find the joys behind it as well.

SMOKE BUSH ARRANGEMENT

The foliage from the smoke bush tree is interesting and adds a lot to any arrangement, but it is the blooms that are the masterpiece! They look like puffs of smoke in pink and red tones and are beautiful on their own or mixed in with other arrangements. They are around for most of the summer and some of the fall, depending on where you are located.

PLANTS

- Smoke bush

SUPPLIES

- Floral shears
- Large ceramic vessel
- Waterproof tape

FORAGE

1. Cut around ten branches in a mix of heights, choosing some that have just the foliage, but most that have the "smoke."

PREPARE

2. Cut the branches at an angle, removing lower leaves, and place them in water to rehydrate prior to being arranged.

3. Create a grid shape with waterproof tape and fill the vessel with water to the top.

ARRANGE

4. Start by placing two pieces horizontally to the left and right, leaning them on the mouth of the vessel. A third piece can be placed more vertically. This will be the basic shape.

5. Continue to fill in the space and build out the initial shape. The beauty in this arrangement is the simple, well-placed design.

DISPLAY AND CARE

6. This arrangement looks best against a wall or backdrop. Make sure to check the water level every few days and refresh as needed.

ETHEREAL HONEYSUCKLE ARRANGEMENT

There are few things I love more than honeysuckle. It has it all: a beautiful shape, soft but colorful greens, blooms that range in beautiful neutral colors and a heavenly scent, and it grows nearly anywhere! I could elaborate on the wonders of honeysuckle, but I would rather you discover it yourself. This arrangement is a lovely way to become acquainted with it.

PLANTS

- Honeysuckle vine
- Porcelain berry vine
- Pittosporum

SUPPLIES

- Floral shears
- Bucket
- Floral foam
- Knife
- Small vase

FORAGE

1. Cut a handful of each green. All that is needed is short, petite handfuls of each. Any greenery that is light and creates movement will look great in this style of arrangement. Just avoid anything with thick, woody stems.

PREPARE

2. Trim the stems at an angle, and put them in clean water so they can drink prior to being arranged.

3. Fill a bucket with water and place the foam on top of the water. Be careful not to submerge it; just let it float and naturally soak up the water. After the foam has sunk to the bottom and darkened, use a knife to cut it to size and place it in the small vase.

(continued)

4

ARRANGE

4–5. Insert the first three pieces of the honeysuckle in an upside-down triangle. Continue to flesh out the shape with more honeysuckle.

6–7. Once the arrangement is full, begin to add the accentuating pieces throughout the arrangement. I chose some porcelain berry vine to add some texture and pittosporum to add some dimensional color.

DISPLAY AND CARE

8. This petite friend is so cute in a nook around the house. The foam should be lightly watered every few days through the life of the arrangement.

IN GOOD COMPANY: WOODLAND FERNS

I love the interest ferns provide to an arrangement. The different textures, shapes and color tones are always an exciting addition. This is a lovely opportunity to let them shine.

PLANTS

- Button fern
- Crispy wave fern
- Japanese fern

SUPPLIES

- Floral shears
- Wire cutter
- Chicken wire
- Waterproof tape
- Stone compote

FORAGE

1. If you are lucky to find ferns growing in the wild, make sure you take advantage of that source. Mine were cut from a cultivated source. Whatever your source is, cut around ten pieces of each type of fern.

PREPARE

2. Trim the stems at an angle, and put them in clean water so they can drink prior to being arranged.

3. With a wire cutter, cut a square of chicken wire twice the size of the compote opening, roll it into a ball and place it inside the compote. Put a piece of waterproof tape across the top of the stone compote to keep the chicken wire in place and fill the compote almost to the top with water.

Note: The stems of the ferns are too delicate for foam.

(continued)

4

ARRANGE

4–6. While designing, keep in mind that the overall shape of the arrangement will be more horizontal due to the shape of the ferns. While they could be placed more vertically, it would not be natural and would look quite odd. Start by placing the Japanese fern in the stone compote, fanning out from the center. Once you have created a base layer and covered up much of the chicken wire, insert the crispy wave fern around the rim of the compote. To finish, add a few pieces of button fern with some wispy bits floating above the arrangement.

DISPLAY AND CARE

7. I like to display this piece in my entryway or in my home office. It adds an element of cheerfulness and renewal. Display this floral design wherever you can best enjoy it. Refresh the water every few days.

PETITE WILDFLOWER ARRANGEMENT

As the weather starts to warm up, little flowers and grasses pop up all over the place. Rather than seeing them as a menace, enjoy the opportunity to have an abundance of cute cut flowers. Have fun with them and create something to brighten up your home! I did not know most of what I was cutting until I looked it up afterward. Do not be deterred by the unknown, but rather embrace it.

PLANTS

- Honeysuckle
- Wild grasses
- Red clover blossoms
- Groundsel (old-man-in-the-Spring)
- Common violet

SUPPLIES

- Floral shears
- Small pitcher
- Waterproof tape (optional)

FORAGE

1. Cut around ten stems of honeysuckle or another green vine. Cut stems of other plants in a mix of shorter heights, around five stems per type.

PREPARE

2. Trim the honeysuckle and remove any leaves that fall below the waterline. Cut the stems at an angle and place them in water to rehydrate prior to being arranged.

3. Fill the pitcher nearly to the top with water. You could create a grid with waterproof tape, but the mouth of the pitcher I used was quite small, so I chose to work without one.

(continued)

ARRANGE

4–6. Arrange pieces of the honeysuckle mostly out toward the left and right with some shorter pieces coming out toward the front. Add five to seven pieces of wild grass in a fan shape. Add a cluster of red clover on one side of the arrangement. Add a cluster of groundsel on the opposite side. Mix in a few more pieces of grass and finish off with a few pieces of common violet.

DISPLAY AND CARE

7. Arrangements like this little guy always look best in little nooks around the house. Refresh the water every couple of days.

POKEWEED WITH CRAPE MYRTLE BLOSSOMS

Weeds get a bad rap. They are viewed as valueless and undesirable, but in reality they are just something that was not cultivated. Once you change the way you look at them, you will see a new wealth of foraging material. Pokeweed is one of my favorites to use in the summer. It has a wonderful shape, a beautiful green hue and lasts for a long time if it's in clean water.

PLANTS

- Pokeweed
- Crape myrtle blossoms in varying colors

SUPPLIES

- Floral shears
- Wire cutter
- Chicken wire
- Waterproof tape
- Garden urn

FORAGE

1. Cut the pokeweed from the base of the stalk, and get it in water immediately. Cut around ten pieces of crape myrtle no longer than 3 feet (91.5 cm) in varying shades. Other greens could easily be used in place of the pokeweed, but there is nothing that moves quite like pokeweed.

PREPARE

2. Clean up the pokeweed stalk by separating it into smaller pieces and put them in clean water.

3. With a wire cutter, cut a square of chicken wire twice the size of the urn opening, roll it into a ball and place it in the urn. Put a piece of waterproof tape across the top of the urn to keep the chicken wire in place. Fill the urn almost to the top with water once prepared.

(continued)

ARRANGE

4–6. Start with two pieces of pokeweed with many offshoots. The pokeweed has such great shape that it does the work for you. Make sure there are high and low points, but also allow it to go a little crazy. Once the pokeweed is filled in, start adding the crape myrtle in an ombré effect from light to dark, working with the existing shape.

DISPLAY AND CARE

7. This statement arrangement looks fabulous in an entryway. Refresh the water every few days.

Note: Pokeweed is poisonous if ingested, so be cautious if you have children or pets.

WILDFLOWER ARRANGEMENT

When there is an abundance of beautiful flowers growing outside, it is easy to create exquisite arrangements with very little material. This is a fun, quick arrangement that you can put together when you want to impress guests without doing a lot of work.

PLANTS

- Stonecrop foliage
- Honeysuckle
- Wild cosmos

SUPPLIES

- Floral shears
- Terra-cotta compote
- Silicon (optional)
- Bucket
- Floral foam
- Knife

FORAGE

1. Because all the ingredients for this arrangement are on the smaller side, forage a little more than you think you will need. Use around ten to fifteen of each stem. Daisies or other small blooms work well if cosmos are unavailable.

PREPARE

2. Trim the branches at an angle, and put them in clean water so they can drink prior to being arranged.

3. Many terra-cotta garden vessels are porous and not watertight, so make sure yours does not leak prior to using. If it is not watertight, pick up some silicon from the local hardware store and brush a light layer on the interior. This will prevent any leakage.

4. Fill a bucket with water and place the foam on top of the water. Be careful not to submerge it; just let it float and naturally soak up the water. After the foam has sunk to the bottom and darkened, use a knife to cut it to size and place it in the compote.

(continued)

5

ARRANGE

5–7. Start by adding the stonecrop to the foam. Once your desired shape is created, fill in with the honeysuckle or another vine, keeping in mind you want a subtle, loose horizontal shape with a few pieces placed a little more vertically. Fill in any holes with honeysuckle, continuing to bring out the existing shape and add a little wildness. Lastly, add some wild cosmos blooms to enhance the arrangement.

DISPLAY AND CARE

8. This style of arrangement is nice in a nook by itself or grouped with other little arrangements. The foam should be lightly watered every few days, and the arrangement should last about a week.

SUMMER GRASSES

This arrangement reminds me of fields in the summer and running wild and free. The addition of the dark foliage in this arrangement adds some interest and depth in an otherwise light and airy form.

PLANTS

- Chinese fringe bush
- Burning bush
- Queen Anne's lace
- Sweet clover
- Wild grass

SUPPLIES

- Floral shears
- Terra-cotta pot
- Silicon (optional)
- Bucket
- Floral foam
- Knife

FORAGE

1. For the base greens, I chose two different types of foliage, Chinese fringe bush and burning bush, but this look could also be accomplished with just one varietal. I love the variation of color in each leaf. The darker tones in the foliage really bring out the color of the Queen Anne's lace seed pods. A total of ten to fifteen stems of foliage are more than enough. Also cut ten to fifteen stems of sweet clover and Queen Anne's lace, and a handful of wild grasses.

PREPARE

2. Trim the branches and stems at an angle, and put them in clean water so they can drink prior to being arranged.

3. Many terra-cotta garden pots are porous and not watertight, so make sure yours does not leak prior to using. If it is not watertight, pick up some silicon from the local hardware store and brush a light layer on the interior. This will prevent any leakage.

4. Fill a bucket with water and place the foam on top of the water. Be careful not to submerge it; just let it float and naturally soak up the water. After the foam has sunk to the bottom and darkened, use a knife to cut it to size and place it in the pot. Because of the shape of the pot, the foam is inconspicuous, so cover-up is not an issue.

(continued)

ARRANGE

5–8. Start by placing the fringe bush foliage in your pot, fanning it out and having it touch the top of the pot, as well as creating a high and a low point. Add the grasses into a similar shape, continuing to fan them out from the pot. Then add the sweet clover in a similar pattern. While the sweet clover has a shape and size similar to that of the grasses, it adds lightness to the arrangement. The last step is to add the Queen Anne's lace. Some pieces can be placed higher in the arrangement, and others can be tucked down low. When I foraged mine, some of it was going to seed, so I chose to mix those with the blooming stems. I chose to cluster them to make more of an overall impact.

DISPLAY AND CARE

9. This style of arrangement is nice in a nook by itself or grouped with other smaller arrangements. The foam should be lightly watered every few days.

TRUMPET VINE ARRANGEMENT

This wild vine is a favorite in the summer. It is easy to work with and quite resilient. It is also great as a solo ingredient because it has so much going on in each stem. There are so many options for what you can make with this colorful vine.

PLANTS

- Trumpet vine

SUPPLIES

- Floral shears
- Waterproof tape
- Footed bronze vessel

FORAGE

1. Cut five pieces of the trumpet vine in varying heights, the longest being at least 3 feet (92 cm). Honeysuckle could be substituted for a simpler arrangement, but then look for another plant to add interest.

PREPARE

2. Trim the branches and stems at an angle, and put them in clean water so they can drink prior to being arranged.

3. Create a grid across the top of the vessel with waterproof tape to help the stems have somewhere to rest. Fill almost to the top with water.

ARRANGE

4. Begin with two pieces of the trumpet vine on either side, creating an exaggerated checkmark shape. Add a few more pieces to flesh out the shape and add life to the arrangement. You can keep this arrangement simple and minimal, or you can continue adding more stems, creating a statement. This type of arrangement is most interesting when it is allowed to float in the vase.

DISPLAY AND CARE

5. This piece would look gorgeous on a table in a sunroom or on a kitchen island. Refresh the water every few days.

WILD GRASSES IN A PITCHER

I love how old-fashioned this arrangement feels. I imagine someone centuries ago foraging and creating something like this for their home. It still feels relevant today!

PLANTS

- Sweet clover
- Wild grasses
- Queen Anne's lace

SUPPLIES

- Floral shears
- Waterproof tape
- Pitcher

FORAGE

1. Cut two handfuls of sweet clover, and one handful of wispy wild grasses and Queen Anne's lace.

PREPARE

2. Trim the stems at an angle, and put them in clean water so they can drink prior to being arranged.

3. Place waterproof tape across the top of the pitcher in a grid to help the stems have somewhere to rest. Fill the pitcher with water.

ARRANGE

4. Create an inverted triangle as your base. I used the sweet clover because it fills the space without weighing down the arrangement. Then add some pieces of the grass while leaving the blades on the stem. I love how they pop against the sweet clover. Finish by adding some blooming Queen Anne's lace, creating high and low points peppered throughout the arrangement.

DISPLAY AND CARE

5. This arrangement would be just darling in a kitchen nook. Refresh the water every few days.

WILD BERRY ARRANGEMENT

The wildness of this arrangement is the epitome of summer. Wild berries and fruits are growing wherever you look. This piece reminds me of the summer holidays, exploring the outdoors and enjoying all the beauty that summer has to offer.

PLANTS

- Porcelain berry vine in different stages of growth
- Wild blackberries

SUPPLIES

- Floral shears
- Terra-cotta pot
- Silicon (optional)
- Bucket
- Floral foam
- Knife

FORAGE

1. The porcelain vine will have many offshoots, so cut longer pieces that can then be cut into smaller pieces, around ten pieces total. If a porcelain vine is unavailable, another vine could be used, but you may want to find another textural element to add to the arrangement. A small amount of the wild blackberry will make an impact. Be careful of its thorns.

PREPARE

2. Trim the branches at an angle, and put them in clean water so they can drink prior to being arranged. Cut off as many thorns as you can before arranging. It may be wise to wear gloves.

3. Many terra-cotta garden pots are porous and not watertight, so make sure yours does not leak prior to using. If it is not watertight, pick up some silicon from the local hardware store and brush a light layer on the interior. This will prevent any leakage.

4. Fill a bucket with water and place the foam on top of the water. Be careful not to submerge it; just let it float and naturally soak up the water. After the foam has sunk to the bottom and darkened, use a knife to cut it to size and place it in the pot. Because of the shape of the vessel, the foam is inconspicuous, so covering up is less of an issue.

(continued)

ARRANGE

5–7. Start by placing the porcelain vine with berries heavier on one side. Then begin placing the wild blackberries on the lighter side in a cluster. To finish off, add some lighter pieces of the porcelain vine without berries throughout the arrangement.

DISPLAY AND CARE

8. This style of arrangement is nice in a nook by itself or grouped with other smaller arrangements. The foam should be lightly watered every few days.

SIMPLE POKEWEED ARRANGEMENT

One thing I love about pokeweed (aside from the wonderful shape) is the variety of colors you can get in one offshoot. With the beautiful burgundy in the stem, the berries transitioning from white, green and black, and the vibrant green leaves, it gives visual interest without needing much else.

PLANTS

- Pokeweed
- Mountain laurel

SUPPLIES

- Floral shears
- Bucket
- Floral foam
- Knife
- Ceramic vessel

FORAGE

1. Cut five to seven stems of pokeweed in varying heights. Cut a few handfuls of the mountain laurel.

PREPARE

2. Trim the stalks and branches at an angle, and put them in clean water so they can drink prior to being arranged.

3. Fill a bucket with water and place the foam on top of the water. Be careful not to submerge it; just let it float and naturally soak up the water. After the foam has sunk to the bottom and darkened, use a knife to cut it to size and place it in a cup that will rest on top of the vessel. That way you do not need to waste foam.

(continued)

7

ARRANGE

4–6. Create a V with the pokeweed, leaving the offshoots on to get the most out of each stem. Add more pieces to exaggerate the shape. In the center and front, add some of the mountain laurel to accentuate the vibrant green leaves of the pokeweed.

DISPLAY AND CARE

7. This arrangement should be displayed on a mantelpiece or somewhere high. It needs to be put out of reach of small children and animals since pokeweed is toxic if ingested. The foam can be lightly watered every few days throughout the life of the arrangement.

PETITE CERAMIC VASES ARRANGEMENT

When it comes to beauty, less is often more. With these little vases, that is absolutely true. One of the most exciting things about bud vases is how many ways they can be mixed and how the plants you choose can be personalized specifically to your design. Think outside the box with what you forage to create a truly special arrangement.

PLANTS

- Smilax
- Pittosporum
- Abelia

SUPPLIES

- Floral shears
- Small ceramic vases

FORAGE

1. Cut a small handful of each green. The smilax will have many offshoots, so one long piece can yield many shorter pieces. Other vines and more delicate greenery can easily be substituted.

PREPARE

2. Trim the stems at an angle, and put them in clean water so they can drink prior to being arranged.

3. Fill the vases almost to the top with water.

ARRANGE

4. Place three pieces of smilax in each vase so they are resting on the top, almost trailing down the vase. Then add a few pieces of pittosporum toward one side. Finish by adding some abelia to the same side as the pittosporum.

DISPLAY AND CARE

5. A cluster of these with some candles makes a beautiful tablescape. Top off the water every few days.

IN GOOD COMPANY: GREENERY STEALS THE SHOW

This is one of those arrangements that is more interesting without blooms. You can really focus on the individual types of greenery and allow your eyes to travel through the different moments within the greenery without any distraction. When you're foraging, pick the greens that interest you most and see what kind of magic you create.

PLANTS

- Mountain laurel foliage
- Chinese privet shrub
- Porcelain berry vine
- Honeysuckle vine

SUPPLIES

- Floral shears
- Bucket
- Floral foam
- Knife
- Footed vase

FORAGE

1. Cut a handful of each green. Most of these are delicate, but the mountain laurel really grounds them. Another hardy shrub would work just as well.

PREPARE

2. Trim the branches and stems at an angle, and put them in clean water so they can drink prior to being arranged.

3. Fill a bucket with water and place the foam on top of the water. Be careful not to submerge it; just let it float and naturally soak up the water. After the foam has sunk to the bottom and darkened, use a knife to cut it to size and place it in the vase.

(continued)

7

ARRANGE

4–6. Insert three to five pieces of mountain laurel into the foam, creating a V. Continue filling out the shape with the Chinese privet. The privet adds some nice texture and a different style of leaf. Continue filling with the honeysuckle, a great choice because of the slightly lighter green tones. Add a few pieces of the porcelain berry vine flowing down the front. Finish with a few of the woody bits from the honeysuckle to the left side. Notice how they balance out the weight of the right side.

DISPLAY AND CARE

7. I love this sort of arrangement on a side table. The foam should be lightly watered every few days.

IN GOOD COMPANY: HERBS

Herbs are useful for more than adding flavor to your favorite foods. They have wonderful movement, an amazing scent and a long duration if left in water. Play with your favorite scents, textures and colors to make this arrangement personal to you.

PLANTS

- Ornamental oregano
- Rosemary
- Italian oregano
- Purple Thai basil
- Lavender

SUPPLIES

- Floral shears
- Terra-cotta compote
- Silicon (optional)
- Wire cutter
- Chicken wire
- Waterproof tape

FORAGE

1. Cut a handful of each herb. These will most likely come from a cultivated source, like an herb garden.

PREPARE

2. Trim the stems at an angle, and put them in clean water so they can drink prior to being arranged.

3. Many terra-cotta compotes are porous and not watertight, so make sure yours does not leak prior to using. If it is not watertight, pick up some silicon from the local hardware store and brush a light layer on the interior. This will stop any leakage from happening.

4. With a wire cutter, cut a square of chicken wire twice the size of the compote opening, roll it into a ball, and place it inside the compote. Put a piece of waterproof tape across the top of the compote to keep the chicken wire in place and fill the compote almost to the top with water.

(continued)

ARRANGE

5–9. Start with two bundles of ornamental oregano on the left and right sides of the arrangement. Fill the center of the arrangement with sprigs of rosemary. Add little bits of Italian oregano spilling out of the sides. Add a few pieces of purple Thai basil in the center of the arrangement to help disperse the color throughout. Finish off with a few pieces of lavender popping out of the arrangement.

DISPLAY AND CARE

10. This arrangement is lovely in a kitchen, small bedroom or powder room. Refresh the water every few days.

LUSH WOODEN PLATTER ARRANGEMENT

When I designed this arrangement, I wanted to create something simple and light with lots of movement. This arrangement's purpose is to be a focal piece while not distracting from table conversation. When creating a shape like this, think out, not up, and allow it to flow.

PLANTS

- Honeysuckle
- Lavender
- Ornamental oregano

SUPPLIES

- Floral shears
- Bucket
- Floral foam
- Knife
- Oval wooden rectangular platter
- Plastic sheet (optional)

FORAGE

1. Cut the honeysuckle into smaller pieces ranging from 6 inches (15 cm) to 3 feet (92 cm). Clean the cuttings by removing any dead leaves or any leaves that will be below the floral foam. Another vine would work well if honeysuckle is unavailable. The lavender and ornamental oregano will most likely need to be cut from a cultivated source, such as an herb garden.

PREPARE

2. Trim the branches and stems at an angle, and put them in clean water so they can drink prior to being arranged.

3. Fill a bucket with water and place the foam on top of the water. Be careful not to submerge it; just let it float and naturally soak up the water. After the foam has sunk to the bottom and darkened, use a knife to cut it to size and place it in the platter, keeping a low profile so it does not take away from the overall look of the arrangement. With an open arrangement like this, the more foam you use, the more you have to cover up! If the platter is not watertight, make sure to line it with plastic to keep it from being damaged or leaking onto the table.

(continued)

ARRANGE

4–5. Begin placing the honeysuckle strategically in the foam. The first pieces you place should be larger and longer to build out the shape. Place some pieces deeper in the foam while others are further out, creating dimension and interest. Work with the natural direction of the stem, rather than trying to fight the shape just to get coverage of your floral foam. You can fill holes with smaller trimmings later after the shape is constructed. This will ensure the foam is concealed while still keeping the arrangement light. I used the platter as my guide for the shape. I started with 2- to 3-foot (61- to 92-cm) pieces and then added shorter pieces. I used approximately twenty pieces total.

6–7. To add a little bit of color and variety, insert the ornamental oregano and lavender sprinkled throughout the arrangement.

DISPLAY AND CARE

8. This arrangement is the perfect centerpiece on the dining room table for a dinner party with friends or family. It is long-lasting. Every couple of days, remove it from the table and lightly water the foam. Be sure the bottom of the platter is completely dry prior to putting it back to ensure it does not get the table wet.

ORNAMENTAL OREGANO HALF WREATH

I love the nontraditional aspects of this wreath. It adds interest and simplicity wherever it is placed and can be used year-round with a myriad of options in foliage. And why not have wreathes other times of the year besides the holidays?

PLANTS

- Ornamental oregano

SUPPLIES

- Floral shears
- Scissors
- Thin wire
- Garden twine

FORAGE

1. I have a confession to make. The oregano I used came from a cultivated source that I luckily had access to, and it was too pretty not to use. You could substitute this with anything that dries well. To test whether something dries well, leave it out of water for a day or two. You are looking for something that gets crispy or hardens rather than something that wilts. You should only need five pieces. Use more if you want more flexibility with each piece or plan to make it longer.

PREPARE

2. Gather all your supplies and create a pile of the oregano. You will be using both hands, so keep everything close and easily accessible.

(continued)

ARRANGE

3–7. Layer each piece facing the same direction and then wire them together from the middle of the stem downward. The top pieces may flatten out the bottom pieces. To avoid this issue, turn the oregano to see how each side will lay best without squishing the others. Keep in mind that this will go against a flat surface, so you will want all of your movement facing forward or to the side. Once the wreath is as long as desired, tie the garden twine around the two ends of the wreath. This also helps cover any wire visible to the naked eye. The garden twine is about twice the length of the wreath.

DISPLAY AND CARE

8. This wreath can be displayed where pictures hang, on a door or anywhere else you see fit.

Fall

Autumn is a special time of year, and the excitement I feel in the spring returns when I see the color variations beginning to form in the leaves. This is an opportunity to let the movement of a vine speak to you or the ridged nature of a branch inspire you to create an austere line. Foliage is also great for beginners because it performs many design tasks in the arrangement. An understanding of foliage—the way it moves, the shapes it creates—allows designers to replicate nature in their arrangements, no matter the ingredients you use.

GOLDEN EMBER ARRANGEMENT

This arrangement is proof that one can create a stunning botanical design without flowers. It has a depth that surpasses all the seasons. Its rich textures and intricate lines create a delicate piece that livens up any household. Find plants that excite you every time you see them; that is sometimes just as fun as the actual arranging!

PLANTS

- Ninebark
- Viburnum berries
- Smoke bush foliage and "smoke"

SUPPLIES

- Wire cutter
- Floral shears
- Chicken wire
- Ceramic urn
- Waterproof tape

FORAGE

1. Cut five pieces of the ninebark, a couple of handfuls of the viburnum berry branches and a few handfuls of the smoke bush with the foliage. The ninebark has a beautiful dark tone in the leaves that mimics the smoke bush foliage, which makes it more interesting than the typical green tones.

PREPARE

2. Trim the branches and stems at an angle, and put them in clean water so they can drink prior to being arranged.

3. With the wire cutter, cut a square of chicken wire twice the size of the urn opening, roll it into a ball and place it inside the urn. Put a piece of waterproof tape across the top of the urn to keep the chicken wire in place and fill the urn almost to the top with water.

(continued)

ARRANGE

4–7. Start with the ninebark with one offshoot to the left and a taller offshoot to the right, stair-stepping shorter pieces down to the top of the bowl. Place the viburnum berry branches with the foliage in an upward diagonal line starting low on the left side and working your way to the right side while also filling in a little bit at the bottom. Lastly, fill the piece with the smoke bush. Starting with an upside-down triangle, add one last piece on the left side to give color, balance and height.

DISPLAY AND CARE

8. This piece is perfect for a mantelpiece or sitting against a wall. Refresh the water every few days.

LARGE-SCALE AUTUMNAL ARRANGEMENT

One of the most exciting events is the changing of fall leaves. I love bringing them inside and playing with them. You can arrange with a rainbow of colors, and the festiveness of the season will be brought out in your home.

PLANTS

- Maple foliage
- Beech foliage
- Dogwood foliage
- Burning bush
- Crape myrtle foliage
- Additional small-leaf foliage, as needed
- Roses (optional)

SUPPLIES

- Floral shears
- Bucket
- Floral foam
- Knife
- Urn

4

FORAGE

1. Gather a selection of foliage ranging in size, shape and hue. To showcase autumn, a mix of red, yellow, orange and even some brown and green, are good colors to start. For this arrangement, the more vibrant the better, as it will create a beautiful contrast in the arrangement. It is also nice to include leaves with multiple tones of color, which often creates a dappled effect.

2. The branches should be at least 3 feet (91.5 cm) long; they can always be trimmed later. Stems should be ½ inch (1 cm) or less in diameter, otherwise they will be too heavy and create issues when arranging. Aim to have five to seven of each type of foliage you collect. The more variety you have, the less you will need of each branch.

PREPARE

3. Organize the foliage by type and "edit" the branches by removing any leaves or stems that will not be visible or will get in the way of the arrangement structure. This will allow for easy placement later.

4. Fill a bucket with water and place the foam on top of the water. Be careful not to submerge it; just let it float and naturally soak up the water. After the foam has sunk to the bottom and darkened, use a knife to cut it to size and place it in the bottom of the urn.

(continued)

ARRANGE

5. To start the arrangement, take the branches with the largest leaves. They will be your focal point and help create the shape and structure of the arrangement. Arrange groups with an odd number of branches to help keep the arrangement asymmetrical. To create a natural look, establish a high point on one side and a low point on the other to form balance. Add a third point coming out toward the front of the arrangement to create dimension.

My largest leaves were the maple, so I began by adding three stems ranging from 2 to 3 feet (50.0 to 91.5 cm) long to the urn and arranged them in a triangle shape to create the main structure.

6. Next, take several branches of another color and size, and use them to fill in the shape and build depth. I took three branches of beech and tucked them around the maple a little closer toward the center.

7. Now take several stems of a third variety of leaf if you have it, or continue to use the branches from the previous step, and fill in the middle and low points so that no foam shows. I used about three branches of dogwood.

8–9. As a finishing touch and to add some final dimension, add a branch with vibrant, but smaller leaves (around 1 to 2 inches [2.5 to 5 cm] in length). I filled in with burning bush, crape myrtle and another small leaf.

10. To take it to the next level, roses or other flowers can be added. However, this is not necessary for a beautiful arrangement.

DISPLAY AND CARE

11. Once you are pleased with your arrangement, you can
    find a beautiful place to display it. I love to showcase
    large-scale arrangements on mantles or entryway tables.
    Find somewhere it can really shine. To extend the life of
    the arrangement, the foam can be lightly watered from
    the top of the arrangement every few days. The leaves
    may slowly fall off or start to get crispy, just like they
    do outside, but embrace those changes and allow the
    arrangement to age naturally.

GOLDEN RAIN ARRANGEMENT

When designing, allow yourself to play with unique elements every now and then. It creates a different look and gives you the opportunity to stretch your skills and get outside of your comfort zone. And in the end, you get a really cool arrangement. In this arrangement, I use golden rain pods, which have a unique way of draping and are fun to use.

PLANTS

- Golden rain foliage
- Golden rain pods
- Pokeweed
- Hydrangea

SUPPLIES

- Floral shears
- Alum
- Wire cutter
- Chicken wire
- Medium-size urn
- Waterproof tape

FORAGE

1. Gather three medium-size bunches each of golden rain foliage and pods, pokeweed and hydrangea at varying lengths but no longer than 3 feet (91.5 cm).

PREPARE

2. Trim the branches and stems at an angle, and put them in clean water so they can drink prior to being arranged. Allow the hydrangea to drink for at least an hour before you start to arrange. Prior to arranging, dip the bottom of the hydrangea stems in ½ inch (1 cm) of alum (a powder found in the spice section of the grocery store). This will help extend its life.

3. With a wire cutter, cut a square of chicken wire twice the size of the urn opening, roll it into a ball and place it in the urn. Put a piece of waterproof tape across the top of the urn to keep the chicken wire in place. Top the urn off with water once prepared.

(continued)

1

ARRANGE

4–8. Start with the golden rain foliage and fan it out in opposite directions, slightly toward the front and back. Continue to build out the greenery, leaving spots to build out the other ingredients. Begin to cluster golden rain pods to one side of the arrangement. Add a few pieces of pokeweed in an inverted triangle. Finish off with a cluster of hydrangea on the opposite side of the pods using a mix of small and large blossoms. Notice how the eye is drawn to move from one side of the arrangement to the other with ease.

DISPLAY AND CARE

9. Medium-size arrangements are great because they are versatile and can be used in many different places. This one would look great as a centerpiece on a table. Refresh the water every few days.

5

6

7

8

MAPLE LEAF ARRANGEMENT

One of my favorite ways to display foliage in my house is simply in a glass jug. This type of arrangement doesn't take long to put together, can be mixed with jugs of various sizes and is long-lasting. It is an elegant statement. It is easy to overlook the beauty of simplicity, but less is definitely more. For a more complex arrangement, other foliage could be mixed in as well.

PLANTS
- Maple branches

SUPPLIES
- Floral shears
- Glass jugs in varying sizes

4

FORAGE

1. Cut around five maple branches in varying heights for the large jug, plus more if you plan to fill more jugs.

PREPARE

2. Trim the branches at an angle, and put them in clean water so they can drink prior to being arranged.

3. Fill the jug to the top with water.

ARRANGE

4. Start by placing one branch about one and a half times the size of the jug. It is easier if you find one with a natural bend, that way you can easily get it to stay horizontal. Place a shorter piece on the opposite side to help balance it out. Place the last few pieces in the center area and more vertically to fill out the shape.

DISPLAY AND CARE

5. This maple arrangement makes a great statement upon entering any room. It looks best front and center. Top it off with water every few days.

SWEET MAPLE BRANCH ARRANGEMENT

One day on a walk after dinner with my husband and our two dogs, we spotted a gorgeous maple tree along the path. I couldn't resist cutting a few of the lovely branches and using them. I love to use maple branches in my arrangements during the late summer and early fall because of the interesting texture and color of the seedpods. They add such a unique quality to any arrangement. Keep an eye out wherever you go, and you will undoubtedly find new types of foraging materials and amazing sources.

PLANTS

- Maple branches with seedpods
- Mountain laurel
- Smilax

SUPPLIES

- Floral shears
- Bucket
- Floral foam
- Knife
- Stone vase

FORAGE

1. Cut five to seven maple branches with seedpods, varying in height. Cut five branches of the mountain laurel with some offshoots. Also, cut two long pieces of smilax vine. This arrangement can easily be achieved by using another type of hardy foliage and delicate vine.

PREPARE

2. Trim the branches and stems at an angle, and put them in clean water so they can drink prior to being arranged.

3. Fill a bucket with water and place the foam on top of the water. Be careful not to submerge it; just let it float and naturally soak up the water. After the foam has sunk to the bottom and darkened, use a knife to cut it to size and place it in the stone vase.

(continued)

ARRANGE

4–7. Start by creating a full V, one side higher than the other, with the seeded maple branches. Add a few pieces to the front and the lower back to fill out the V and help cover the foam. The next step is to add some mountain laurel to the sides, mirroring the initial shape of the maple and adding to spots that seem to have holes. Lastly, add some smilax so it's spilling out of the front of the arrangement.

DISPLAY AND CARE

8. This arrangement looks beautiful on a small mantelpiece or by the window. The foam can be lightly watered every few days.

MYRTLE AND VIBURNUM BERRY ARRANGEMENT

I love the mix of tones in this arrangement from the true greens of the myrtle, the yellow and red tones of the viburnum berries, the light puffs of red from the smoke bush and the gradation of colors in the Heuchera. It's a delectable feast for the eyes!

PLANTS

- Myrtle
- Viburnum berry
- Heuchera
- Smoke bush

SUPPLIES

- Floral shears
- Bucket
- Floral foam
- Knife
- Pottery vase

FORAGE

1. The myrtle shrub produces plentiful branches, so you only need to cut a few. Next, cut seven to ten viburnum berry branches or another type of plant that has berries. Lastly, cut a large handful of Heuchera leaves (or another flat leaf) and smoke bush.

PREPARE

2. Trim the branches and stems at an angle, and put them in clean water so they can drink prior to being arranged.

3. Fill a bucket with water and place the foam on top of the water. Be careful not to submerge it; just let it float and naturally soak up the water. After the foam has sunk to the bottom and darkened, use a knife to cut it to size and place it in the vase.

(continued)

ARRANGE

4–8. To start, create a V with the myrtle going diagonally out of the vessel. Fill in the center with shorter pieces of the myrtle to make the V less exaggerated. Then begin to add the Heuchera leaves in an overemphasized manner, pulling some far out and tucking others far in. The next step is to remove all the foliage from the viburnum berries. Then add the berries in a triangle-like pattern, pushing some in, pulling some farther out and tucking some in the center. Lastly, add the smoke bush, putting it near the berries to enhance their color.

DISPLAY AND CARE

9. This arrangement is perfect as a table centerpiece for autumn gatherings with family and friends. The stunning floral arrangement can enhance any table display. The foam can be lightly watered every few days through the life of the arrangement.

GREENERY AND GRASSES ARRANGEMENT

This arrangement was fun and inspiring to me because of the addition of the grass. Most people wouldn't think of putting grass in this style of arrangement. However, using grass is a great choice, especially in the absence of flowers, because it adds a lot of texture and visual interest. This piece is a great example of finding beauty in everyday simplicities and thinking outside the box.

PLANTS

- Smilax
- Honeysuckle
- Variegated pittosporum
- Wild grasses

SUPPLIES

- Floral shears
- Bucket
- Floral foam
- Knife
- Brass goblet

FORAGE

1. Vines are the most important aspect of this arrangement because they keep it delicate. While the variegation of the pittosporum adds new color, it is not necessary, so you can skip pittosporum if it's difficult to find in your area. Due to the petite nature of this floral piece, a handful of each of the listed plants is all that is needed.

PREPARE

2. Trim the stems at an angle, and put them in clean water so they can drink prior to being arranged.

3. Fill a bucket with water and place the foam on top of the water. Be careful not to submerge it; just let it float and naturally soak up the water. After the foam has sunk to the bottom and darkened, use a knife to cut it to size and place it in the brass goblet.

(continued)

ARRANGE

4–7. First, add smilax so it's hanging out of the goblet. Then add the honeysuckle to create a more horizontal shape. Next, add a few pieces of the variegated pittosporum to bring a bit of color variation to the arrangement. Then add the grasses, fanning them out all over the arrangement.

DISPLAY AND CARE

8. You can put this floral piece tucked away in a cozy corner in your house. The foam can be lightly watered every few days through the life of the arrangement.

CHINESE FRINGE ARRANGEMENT WITH BERRIES

Some people think that arrangements need to be elaborate with a wide range of different flowers and greenery, but a floral design can look stunning with only a solitary piece. Remember, there is beauty in minimalism. This arrangement is great when you are short on time and sources, and it still has a big impact in the home.

PLANTS

- Chinese fringe tree

SUPPLIES

- Floral shears
- Waterproof tape
- Silver pitcher

FORAGE

1. Cut three branches of Chinese fringe, around 3 feet (91.5 cm) long each. Another foliage with some textural elements or berries would look great, too!

PREPARE

2. Trim the branches at an angle, and put them in clean water so they can drink prior to being arranged.

3. Create a grid with waterproof tape on the pitcher's opening to help keep the branches in place. Fill the pitcher with water almost to the top.

(continued)

4

ARRANGE

4–6. Take the first branch of the Chinese fringe tree and
place it in the silver pitcher high on the left side. Next,
take the second branch and place it in the pitcher lower
on the right, creating a checkmark shape. Lastly, place the
third piece in the middle of the two branches. This will
create a full design and a stair-step effect, creating a visual
line for the eye to follow.

DISPLAY AND CARE

7. I love to put this arrangement in my kitchen. It adds a bit
of freshness and liveliness. You can put this arrangement
wherever you feel it best complements the interior of your
house. Refresh the water every few days.

Winter

Around the holidays, I love to forage for evergreens to decorate my house. Nothing gets me more into the holiday spirit than the smell of evergreens. They are so wonderful to work with and last for a good long while, even without water. Although they are available year-round, I prefer to let them be special during the winter. Winter also gives us one of my absolute favorite flowers, camellias.

IN GOOD COMPANY: WINTER GREENS ARRANGEMENT

If you find yourself with a little free time around the holidays and want to create something a little more complex, then this arrangement is a perfect choice for you. Your holiday guests will be impressed with the intricate designs of this winter greens arrangement.

PLANTS

- Cedar
- Cypress
- Blue spruce
- Holly with berries
- Evergreen

SUPPLIES

- Floral shears
- Bucket
- Floral foam
- Knife
- Brass compote

FORAGE

1. When I was foraging, I was looking for plants of different sizes and shapes, and those with cones, berries and different color variations. You want to have five different types of winter greens or evergreens, five to ten branches of each. Be careful to have the right amount; too many is distracting and not enough lacks visual inspiration.

PREPARE

2–3. Trim the branches and stems at an angle, and put them in clean water so they can drink prior to being arranged. Keep in mind when trimming the branches to cut little pieces off to expose the bottom of the stem. This will make it easier to place the stem in the floral foam.

4. Fill a bucket with water and place the foam on top of the water. Be careful not to submerge it; just let it float and naturally soak up the water. After the foam has sunk to the bottom and darkened, use a knife to cut it to size and place it in the compote.

(continued)

5

ARRANGE

5. Let's start with a little drama by bringing the height up front and work our way down with this arrangement. The piece of cedar that I chose is great because it not only offers height but also a few offshoots at the bottom to create body in the arrangement. Continue to add the cedar while working at the base of the arrangement to create a horizontal droop. Be sure to leave plenty of space for the other ingredients.

6–8. Next, add a few pieces of cypress. After these pieces have been added, insert blue spruce to fill some of the holes and add a cooler green tone. Then add some holly with berries, if you can find it. I really love holly in this arrangement because it adds a different leaf shape and the berries add a new hue of color to the mix. After the holly, I added a few evergreen branches and a pinecone. I love giving a woodsy look to holiday arrangements.

6

7

DISPLAY AND CARE

9. This piece is a perfect complement to any holiday decoration. The foam should be lightly watered every few days. This arrangement can last you through the entire holiday season and even into the New Year.

8

HOLLY AND IVY ARRANGEMENT WITH POPS OF CAMELLIA

Just because it is cold outside doesn't mean that you cannot have some blossoms in your house. Where I live in Atlanta, Georgia, camellias start to bloom in late fall and are around until early spring. They offer a variety of colors and are a beautiful small flower. You will enjoy collecting and playing with these sweet buds! If you are in a region that has very cold winters, note that it may not be available, so use any other wintry bloom you can find instead, or simply leave it out—the arrangement will still be lovely!

PLANTS

- Tree ivy
- English ivy
- Holly foliage
- Camellia blooms

SUPPLIES

- Floral shears
- Bucket
- Floral foam
- Knife
- Medium-size compote

FORAGE

1. Ivy is quite possibly the easiest plant to forage. It is invasive and grows nearly everywhere. Another great thing about ivy, a little goes a long way. Five to ten pieces will give you plenty of coverage in a medium-size arrangement. A handful of holly and camellia are all that is needed to get a different shape and color to finish off this fun arrangement.

PREPARE

2. Cut the bottom of the stems and put them in clean water so they can drink prior to being arranged.

3. Fill a bucket with water and place the foam on top of the water. Be careful not to submerge it; just let it float and naturally soak up the water. After the foam has sunk to the bottom and darkened, use a knife to cut it to size and place it in the compote.

(continued)

4

ARRANGE

4–6. To start, use a mix of the thinner vine-like pieces of ivy, and then add the fuller, more mature ivy leaves. When creating the shape, include a few defined highs and lows. The ivy has a natural drape, providing great coverage over the vessel. Once the foam is no longer visible, add the holly in a layered line toward the front of the arrangement. It will create a natural area to then add the camellia blooms, continuing to build on that line. Only a few camellia pieces are needed to make an impact.

DISPLAY AND CARE

7. This arrangement is a wonderful holiday centerpiece. The holly and ivy will last well into the one- to two-week range, but the camellia blooms will start to age after a few days. Once the blooms start to look worn down, pull them out and enjoy a simple greenery arrangement. Lightly water the foam every few days to keep things fresh.

SIMPLE HOLLY ARRANGEMENT

The inspiration for this floral design was a cute little tea tin that I had brought back from my last trip to England, and I knew it would be darling as a holiday arrangement. At this time of year, things tend to be hectic, and sometimes the best way to combat craziness is through simplicity. Try to find a special vessel and create this arrangement with it.

PLANTS
- Holly

SUPPLIES
- Floral shears
- Bucket
- Floral foam
- Knife
- Tea tin

4

FORAGE

1. Cut five pieces of the holly and a few extra. When pruning the holly, be careful of the prickly ends. Believe me; blood and arranging do not mix!

PREPARE

2. Trim the branches at an angle, and put them in clean water so they can drink prior to being arranged.

3. Fill a bucket with water and place the foam on top of the water. Be careful not to submerge it; just let it float and naturally soak up the water. After the foam has sunk to the bottom and darkened, use a knife to cut it to size and place it in the tea tin.

ARRANGE

4. Start with one diagonal holly piece coming out of the center to the left. Add the second piece a little lower in the opposite direction. Then add two more pieces to the sides of the arrangement, each shorter than the original piece. Finish with one holly piece in the center.

DISPLAY AND CARE

5. This little guy looks really cute in a kitchen or little nook of the house. Lightly water the foam every few days.

WINTER GREENS IKEBANA ARRANGEMENT

Just because certain things are typically created with evergreens, like wreaths and garlands, doesn't mean that is all they are good for. Have fun with them and get inspired by the shape of a branch. Use them in a unique way, such as I did with this stunning minimalistic arrangement.

PLANTS

- Winter greens

SUPPLIES

- Floral shears
- Small floral frog
- Shallow brass tray
- Putty adhesive or super glue

FORAGE

1. Find a selection of draping winter evergreen branches. Only three pieces are required for this arrangement, but gather a few extras so you have options. The longest piece should be no longer than 3 feet (91.5 cm).

PREPARE

2. Adhere the floral frog to the brass tray. For a less permanent option, waterproof putty is a great choice. Otherwise, I suggest super glue. Once the frog is secure, fill the tray with a light covering of water.

(continued)

3. Trim your branches to the desired height. When working with a frog, it is sometimes helpful to cut a slit on the bottom of the branch so the pins can hold it more securely. It also helps the branch absorb more water. In ikebana style of floral arranging, the overall height can vary. Typically, the tallest is one and a half times the size of the vessel, the brass tray in this case. This piece represents heaven. The second piece is three-quarters the size of the first and represents Earth. The final piece is three-quarters the size of the second and represents humans.

ARRANGE

4–6. First, add the piece representing Earth to the right. Continue to arrange the pieces like a tripod, one going diagonally to the left, one diagonally and slightly toward the back on the right, and one diagonally and slightly toward the front on the right. If the frog is still visible, use a few small pieces to cover it up.

DISPLAY AND CARE

7. This sort of arrangement needs a space without many distractions. It works well on a side table against a wall or in front of a window. Make sure the stems are covered with water and refresh every few days.

ELAEAGNUS INSTALLATION

You can find Elaeagnus *growing in abundance, much to the dismay of many gardeners. They dislike* Elaeagnus *for the same reasons I adore it. It is easy to use in many different arrangements. Find a space in your environment that wants to have an epic arrangement and let it shine.*

PLANTS

- *Elaeagnus* (silverberry)

SUPPLIES

- Floral shears
- Bucket
- Floral foam
- Knife
- Rectangular vessel

FORAGE

1. For this arrangement, you will need to cut at least twenty pieces of the *Elaeagnus*. I recommend cutting more than you think is needed. Try to cut longer pieces since they can be cut shorter later on. When cutting *Elaeagnus*, be careful because new growth can sometimes be thorny.

PREPARE

2. Trim the branches at an angle, and put them in clean water so they can drink prior to being arranged.

3. Fill a bucket with water and place the foam on top of the water. Be careful not to submerge it; just let it float and naturally soak up the water. After the foam has sunk to the bottom and darkened, use a knife to cut it to size and place it in the vessel.

(continued)

ARRANGE

4–7. To begin, start with a few pieces of *Elaeagnus* going up vertically and a few pieces horizontally, slightly toward the front. Next, work from the center, adding a stair-step between the two pieces diagonally. Continue to fill in the arrangement. As you go, make sure to add pieces facing backward so you can see the beautiful silver color of the leaves. Take a large piece and place it diagonally toward the left. Add a few more pieces of *Elaeagnus* going out toward the left, and you have a finished arrangement.

DISPLAY AND CARE

8. This arrangement is lovely in front of a fireplace or framing the opening of a doorway. The foam can be lightly watered every few days, and the arrangement can possibly last weeks, depending on the hardiness of the *Elaeagnus*.

SMALL CAMELLIA ARRANGEMENT

On a winter trip to the gardens of Middleton Place in Charleston, South Carolina, the first place camellias were cultivated in the United States, I became intimately acquainted with these stunning blooms. These shrubs were gigantic, towering over my petite frame. After that experience, I began to notice camellias more frequently, and our love affair has continued to grow. This arrangement creates the perfect amount of brightness on a blustery winter day.

PLANTS

- Pittosporum
- Camellia

SUPPLIES

- Floral shears
- Bucket
- Floral foam
- Knife
- Small brass bowl

FORAGE

1. Pittosporum is a great foliage to know about. Some varietals are evergreen and quite hardy. It comes in different colors, sizes and weights, and it can be variegated. For this arrangement, ten petite pieces will do well. For the camellias, five to six pieces will make a nice impact. This variety of pittosporum has large, solid leaves that make it extremely hardy, so any other shrub with similar characteristics would work great as a substitute.

PREPARE

2. Cut the bottom of the stems and put them in clean water so they can drink prior to being arranged.

3. Fill a bucket with water and place the foam on top of the water. Be careful not to submerge it; just let it float and naturally soak up the water. After the foam has sunk to the bottom and darkened, use a knife to cut it to size and place it in the brass bowl.

(continued)

4

ARRANGE

4–7. Start with the pittosporum, creating an upside-down tripod on the left with the high point of the arrangement. Then mirror this on the opposite side, creating the low point. Fill in by adding shorter pieces at varying heights so they are on different planes. To accentuate the high and low points, add the camellias in a similar pattern.

DISPLAY AND CARE

8. An arrangement of this size can be used in a small corner or grouped with other smaller arrangements on a dining table. Top the foam off with water every few days.

IN GOOD COMPANY: WINTER GREENS HOLIDAY WREATH

Holiday wreaths are nice because they have a long life span without water. I especially like wreaths because they bring a new variety to ornamental decorations around the holidays.

PLANTS

- Cypress
- Holly with berries
- Cedar
- Bare braches (optional)

SUPPLIES

- Floral shears
- Wreath form
- Wire cutter
- Medium gauge green floral wire

FORAGE

1. When foraging, be on the lookout for different types of winter greens because each will bring something unique to the arrangement. Try to find a variety of sizes and shapes, as well as those with berries and different color variations. You want to have five to ten bunches of each type of winter greens or evergreens.

PREPARE

2. Cut the branches at around 6-inch (15-cm) increments and have a pile of each ingredient ready to use as you design your wreath. When you buy wreath forms, they tend to have multiple-size wire circles combined together. Because I am more minimalistic and did not want a heavy wreath, I chose to cut the form with a wire cutter, and just use the smallest form for my wreath.

ARRANGE

3–7. Start with a cypress branch and delicately wire it onto
the wreath form from the middle of the stem downward.
Once it is almost secure, you can add your next ingredient.
Keep in mind that there are always opportunities to increase
the strength of the wreath design later, so do not stress as
you go. As you continue to wire, add the next ingredient,
the holly. Layer it slightly on top of the cypress. Be careful
not to cover up all the cypress. Next, add some cedar to the
wreath. Make sure to wrap the wire just around the stems.
That way the leaves will not be crushed. Repeat this process
until you cover up the form. A few bare branches can be
added in one principal spot to add an area of central interest.

DISPLAY AND CARE

8. Showcase this wreath proudly on your front door. Spritz
the wreath with water every few days. Evergreens tend to
have a long life span, so this wreath should last through
the whole holiday season.

WINTER HONEYSUCKLE ARRANGEMENT

Once, while foraging for a wedding, I discovered a new green. It was love at first sight. It had a beautiful, rich color, a natural bend in the shape and it was hardy. What more could you ask for? It wasn't until later that I found out it was a varietal of honeysuckle! Always look for new, exciting material. You never know when you'll find your next favorite foliage! This arrangement is as much about the simple greenery as it is about the crisp, white vase. It reminds me of the minimalistic designs that are found in Scandinavia.

PLANTS
- Winter honeysuckle

SUPPLIES
- Floral shears
- White ceramic vase

4

FORAGE

1. Cut five to ten pieces of the winter honeysuckle, at least 2 feet (61 cm) in length. Since little is needed for this arrangement, focus on quality over quantity. Take time to find pieces with the perfect curve or an interesting leaf structure.

PREPARE

2. Trim the stems at an angle, and put them in clean water so they can drink prior to being arranged.

3. Fill the vase with water almost to the top.

ARRANGE

4. Create a very open, loose upside-down triangle. Once that basic shape is created, add a few more pieces to fill out the front and back, placing them low so they do not take away from the overall triangle. Keep the overall design minimal, allowing the vase to shine.

DISPLAY AND CARE

5. I kept this floral piece to the side of my mantle for several weeks, and I was shocked at how good it still looked. Refresh the water every few days.

A Horticultural Guide for Beginners

For many people, being on the constant hunt for the perfect cut item is simply not enough. Once you have some sweat (and maybe a little blood) in the game, you find yourself wanting more than what is sold at the traditional florist or what is found in your neighborhood. You want to understand these plants better, starting right at the beginning, having direct access to them in your own yard. I wrote this section for those of you who want to create beautiful arrangements in your own home from things you have grown. It brings such a great feeling of accomplishment being able to use flowers from your own garden to make an arrangement. Gardening can be a process of trial and error but that is how one learns. Don't be afraid to get in there and get your hands dirty; it's part of the fun.

TIPS FOR CREATING YOUR OWN FORAGING GARDEN

There are certain things that are nice to have access to at all times. Stepping outside your front door and being able to cut botanicals is glorious. I have a terrible habit of compulsively buying plants for my cutting garden, but often not finding time to plant them or the proper place for them to thrive. Discovering the science behind your land is vital in a healthy cutting garden. While there are many plants that flourish without much love or support, it still takes time for them to grow and survive a regular trimming.

There are four important things to keep in mind if you desire to plant: soil, light, water and climate. To start, only a basic knowledge is necessary.

SOIL

Soil can be either acidic or alkaline. Too much of either does not lend well to a plant's development. It is the Goldilocks Paradox; it is important to find soil that is "just right." While we do see plants that thrive without any assistance, this is not always the norm.

Each plant also has certain nutrient needs, just like humans do. Too much or too little of one nutrient will cause health issues in the plant. The basic nutrients that are tracked in the soil are nitrogen, phosphorus and potassium (NPK). Their functions can be easily remembered with this trick: up, down and all around. The nitrogen helps the plants sprout (up). The phosphorus helps the plant build a strong root network (down). Lastly, the potassium helps the plant grow, allowing plenty of foraging opportunities (all around). Kits can be purchased at your local gardening store to test the soil at your home. There are also options to get your soil tested professionally, through an agricultural lab. When you know the state of your soil, you can then talk to your local garden nursery about what types of amendments are needed.

LIGHT

Each plant has a required amount of light it prefers to get on a daily basis, and most nurseries have that listed on the plant or have knowledgeable employees who will gladly help guide you in the right direction. Typically, the amount of light a plant needs can be broken into four categories. Plants that need full sun require over six hours of direct sunlight, preferably between the hours of 9:00 a.m. and 5:00 p.m. Those that need partial sun require between three to six hours of direct sunlight. Plants that require dappled sun need filtered sunlight, typically through the leaves of a tree or larger shrub. Shade-loving plants cannot get more than three hours of sunlight a day or they will begin to scorch. Monitoring your yard or desired garden spot can be challenging due to the sun shifting throughout the year, but looking for the average is all that is required.

WATER

This is self-explanatory, but making sure a plant gets the right amount of moisture is crucial, especially in the beginning of its life. While both underwatered and overwatered plants can look similar at first glance, a closer look will reveal the true state of the plant. If the plant is underwatered, the soil around it will be dry and the leaves crispy. If the plant is overwatered, the soil will be overly damp, and the leaves will be soft and limp. This can lead to root rot, which can ultimately kill the plant.

GUIDE TO THE USDA PLANT ZONES

Each plant thrives in its native environment, and the United States Department of Agriculture (USDA) has come up with a map of different zones within which certain plants flourish. Many other countries have their own version of their zones, which should be accessible through their agricultural department.

While there are more factors to a zone than your exact location on a map, this is a great guide to use and will help you predict whether a plant will do well in your backyard. Most plants live within a range, which is why you can mostly rely on this zone guide. The map measures a plant's hardiness, or the lowest temperature it can survive. Each zone covers 10-degree increments.

NOVICE GUIDE TO THE USDA PLANT ZONES

Zone	Temperature
Zone 1	-60 to -50°F (-51 to -45°C)
Zone 2	-50 to -40°F (-45 to -40°C)
Zone 3	-40 to -30°F (-40 to -34°C)
Zone 4	-30 to -20°F (-34 to -28°C)
Zone 5	-20 to -10°F (-28 to -23°C)
Zone 6	-10 to 0°F (-23 to -17°C)
Zone 7	0 to 10°F (-17 to -12°C)
Zone 8	10 to 20°F (-12 to -6°C)
Zone 9	20 to 30°F (-6 to -1°C)
Zone 10	30 to 40°F (-1 to 4°C)
Zone 11	40 to 50°F (4 to 10°C)

My Foraging Garden Favorites

Elaeagnus. I love *Elaeagnus* because it is so low maintenance and great in many different arrangements.

Abelia. The small, delicate leaves with blooms for part of the year are perfect!

Pittosporum. There are so many different varietals, but my favorite is Italian. The small leaves with the color variation are beautiful and hardy.

Camellia. Though the flowers are available only for a limited time, the foliage is beautiful all year.

Chinese fringe bush (*Loropetalum*). I love the foliage it produces, from green to burgundy, and it is very low maintenance.

SUPPLIES AND TOOLS

CLIPPERS

Clippers are absolutely the most important tool in your arsenal. Just as chefs must take care of their knives, floral designers must care for their clippers and treat them well. I have two must-haves:

1. A basic set of foral shears/clippers. They can be a simple set from the hardware store or a nicer pair bought online. Just make sure they are used only for cutting smaller pieces, otherwise they will dull. Confession: I regularly break this rule because I do not always have loppers with me.

2. A pair of bypass pruners or loppers for foraging larger branches.

WIRE CUTTER

A wire cutter is an essential tool for your kit. Some people are easily tempted to just use their regular clippers for clipping wires; please don't give into this temptation. The wire will quickly damage your clippers, rendering them useless. Invest in a wire cutter; it doesn't have to be fancy, just functional.

CHICKEN WIRE

There are multiple kinds of chicken wire, but the main one I recommend is 1-inch (2.5-cm) poultry netting that you can get at your local hardware store. Or you can also find specific enamel-coated wire from a floral supply store. Both work fine, but be careful when cutting. Freshly cut wire edges are sharp.

PADDLE WIRE

Paddle wire is great for wreaths and garlands and comes in a variety of gauges. The higher the gauge, the thinner the wire. Gauge is often just a preference, but keep in mind how sturdy the material is that you are working with. A heavy gauge can hurt thinner stems.

FLORAL FOAM

Floral foam comes in a variety of sizes and shapes if you buy it from a floral supplier. For all the arrangements in this book, I used the standard brick size, which is also available from any craft store. If you buy from a craft store, make sure it is wet foam rather than dry foam, which is used for silk flower arranging.

FLORAL FROG

Floral frogs are one of my favorite tools for design. They take a little getting used to, but once you get used to them, you won't want to go back. They allow you to directly place each stem in the vessel. With a frog, an initial infrastructure is made and then the stems or branches begin to support themselves.

ACKNOWLEDGMENTS

This book would not have happened without the love and support of some amazing people in my life. I am forever grateful to them for believing in me and supporting me through all my crazy life adventures.

To Paul: My rock. My everything. You're unending support and encouragement allows me to flourish in ways I never dreamed possible.

To Grace: My sweet friend and collaborator. Thank you for your willingness to do whatever is necessary for the photo. Without you, this book would not exist.

To Ashley: My darling sister who helped this book come together by taking my thoughts and ramblings and helping turn them into words. Thank you for constantly reminding me to imagine and create new things.

To my Parents: I bet you never thought the girl who would rather be clean and tidy would become the woman who would be covered in mud, foliage, scrapes or whatever else was necessary to get the perfect branch or flower. Thank you for allowing me to explore and figure out the path that was right for me.

To my Flower Friends: Thank you for constantly sharing your knowledge with me and allowing me to grow in my craft. No man is an island and it is because of all of you that I am where I am. I will never forget that! I hope to always be as gracious to others and help them on their path. There are too many to name, but I would like to send a special thanks to Hannah Evans, Amy Osaba, Mary McLeod, Ashley Beyer, Natalia Scott Perkins, Ashley Woodson Bailey and Scott Shepherd.

Lastly, thank you to Page Street Publishing and all the people who took a chance on me! Without that leap of faith, who knows where I would be?

ABOUT THE AUTHOR

Rebekah Clark Moody is the owner of Forage & Fleur, a floral design company based in Atlanta, Georgia. Rebekah's floral arrangement style is heavily inspired by the beauty of nature. Rebekah has traveled across the United States and internationally, designing floral arrangements for many professional projects. Her work has been featured in many publications, including Style Me Pretty, *The Knot* and *Utterly Engaged*.

INDEX